salmonpoetry

Publishing Irish & International
Poetry Since 1981

Stopgap Grace
Neil McCarthy

Published in 2018 by
Salmon Poetry
Cliffs of Moher, County Clare, Ireland
Website: www.salmonpoetry.com
Email: info@salmonpoetry.com

ISBN 978-1-912561-07-0

COVER ARTWORK: *"Bing" by Jennifer Bada, California, USA*
COVER DESIGN & TYPESETTING: *Siobhán Hutson*

Printed in Ireland by Sprint Print

Salmon Poetry gratefully acknowledges the support of
The Arts Council / An Chomhairle Ealaíon

for Jeanette

Acknowledgements

I am grateful to the editors of the following magazines and journals in which some of the poems in this collection, or versions of the poems, first appeared:

The SHOp (Ireland), *Magma* (UK), *Orbis* (UK), *The Literary Bohemian* (online), *The Cortland Review* (US), *The Toronto Quarterly* (Canada), *Poetry Salzburg Review* (Austria), *SAND* (Germany), *Popshot* (UK), *The Dalhousie Review* (Canada), *The Coachella Review* (online), *Pilvax* (Hungary), *Burning Bush 2* (online), *The Lascaux Review* (online), *The Subterranean Quarterly* (online), *The Galway Review* (online), *Crannóg* (Ireland), *Sveske* (Serbia), *New Planet Cabaret* (Ireland), *Tribuna* (Romania), *Tiuk!* (Romania), *Astra* (Romania), and *The Stockholm Review* (online).

On a personal note, many thanks to Jeanette and Isobel McCarthy (through thick and thin), Stephen Murray, Denisa Duran, Niall Connolly, Russell Thorburn, Graham Smith, Brendan Constantine, David Rynhart, Dominik Nostitz and the Laden crew, Mary Murphy, Robert Hunter Jones, John Tully, and all the event organizers who have put up with me and put me up down the years.

Thank you too to Jessie Lendennie and Siobhán Hutson at Salmon Poetry for all the hard work and support.

Contents

I

II

III

IV

V

I

The Eleventh Commandment

I never thought I'd miss the sound of church bells,
reminding me of my sudden apostasy,
faintly ringing over the hubbub where even the
birds can't get a word in edgeways.

I think of Protestant churches back home and the horse
chestnut trees that guard them, their gravel paths
far less worn than those of their Catholic brethren.
In my memory it's always late October.

Tonight I walked through the big wind, the
unexpected gusts that blasted with pleasure
the street where the palms had shed their garb.
I battled north on Sunset, watched a fire truck
barge its way through the lights on Coronado,
threw my head into a bar before happy hour
ended to find *The Quiet Man* being projected onto
the back wall; just in time to see Seán Thornton's
lean-in-to-kiss and Mary Kate pure as a storm
in the graveyard's alluring loneliness.

Entranced by the projection, I watched the
grainy landscape of my past silently flow
across the wall in Technicolor, disturbed now
and again by the ripple of a passing shadow,
a head-turning siren from the street, the fancy
footwork of the wind jabbing at the door as
Seán Thornton was laid out across the floor.
And I wanted him to be me –

an Irishman walloped by America,
having broken every Commandment, bar one.
And here, though thou shall not complain
about the weather, the sound of traffic drums as
consistently as rain carried in on a south-westerly,
as we hold a finger to our lips
to silence the misguidance of our gods.

This isn't Silverlake anymore

"Send lawyers guns and money, the shit has hit the fan."

Warren Zevon

1.

In another life, I'd run away with the waitress,
scream across Santa Monica Boulevard negligent of red lights.
In another time, I'd perhaps get her to take the wheel
while I shoot out the tyres of the pursuing cop cars,
confident of making the border before nightfall.

We'd lie low in Tijuana, maybe cut and dye each other's hair
and mull over the maps and the madness of our options.
Bolivia might come into the equation, as might Honduras,
which would be less of a drive and warmer at night.
It might then be time to dump the stolen Cadillac.

Back in LA, the news headlines would make my colleagues
giddy with perversion. In a smoky room a phone would ring,
the receiver lift and a voice on the other end announce
in excitement: *Mac's made it!*

2.

Desires crackle like moths to a hot bulb in this café, the
scripts abandoned and the headshots growing older by the day.
They still dress the part mind you, the waitress in her bowler
hat and black bra visible through her thin white cotton blouse;
my neighbour in his striped three-piece suit and pocket
    watch to boot.

I was told about the ice-cream parlour across the street and
I shift my attention, watching the clientele come and go,
when all of a sudden I realise it's not me that's on the run,
    it's you.
And there you are dressed to the nines, dark sunglasses and
    bouncy hair,
men waiting until you have passed before turning to inhale
the slipstream of your perfume –

    – it's Florence. It's early summer. There you are.

In front of a cathedral, pigeons scatter as *Carabinieri* race towards
the bank alarm calling out for help, but you? You just light a
cigarette and toss the match stick over your shoulder. It's all
being shot in black and white don't you know to give it that
    timeless sense,
while from an open balcony window we can hear a cello play
    the Bach
Preludes as the credits roll and you disappear into the foreground.

3.

I'm listening to the slightly scratched voice of Joan Baez
singing about junipers in the pale moonlight,
applause erupting like hailstone on a corrugated iron roof.
I am singing back through the bedroom wall,
wishing the neighbours would just shut up for once and listen.

But night has arrived with its baton, taking its dark lectern on cue
and conducting its flotilla of noise:
police helicopters, fire trucks, ambulances, a car alarm crying
    wolf to the night.

Headlights, red lights, green lights, turning signals, cross-walks
    flashing,
gas station forecourt lights; Sunset Boulevard from this angle
    looks more
like a fallen Christmas tree.

And I am reading your email, throwing my mind back to the
    wine bar
tables where we would arm wrestle over the colours:
misty-memory-green, winter-cheek-red –
each new phrase coined celebrated like a scientific breakthrough.

In another life, I would run away with you,
into the tattoo-blue of early evening, cover our tracks
and burn every single one of those maps.

Bacon

for Dan Swartz

I ate tonight the best hotdog I have ever bitten into,
wrapped in bacon, served in a toasted roll with
caramelised onions and sweet chilli,
            thick as an iron gutter pipe.

I hated every bite, bitter in the knowledge is was
costing me eight dollars plus tax;

the fact it had been slid in my direction across the table
by a tattooed arm attached to a man in a
baseball hat who shook his fist and told me
that my choice was *awesome*.

I like to taste effort in what I consider awesome;
to suffer penance through hunger and wait.
I blasted back to the *lángos* I ate after a three hours
straight as a passenger on the back seat of a car
with no seatbelts,
            shuddering through Miskolc in the direction
of Szalonna.

You told me the latter translated as bacon, and I smirked
at the irony, but bit my tongue and helped unpack
while you took the gypsy-proofing off the house,
chopped the wood, aired the flumes, lit the fires,
crushed the garlic, vacuumed the larvae from the
window sills, fixed the beds in advance, fried the
lángos and opened the *palinka*.

We ate that night the best bread I had ever bitten into,
not before bowing our heads in awe
            to the spirit's holy gospel.

A Selection of Cured Meats and Jesus

'Pearl' is by and large the greatest name for a
street that I have ever received a parking ticket on,
and who'd have thought we'd be here; that we'd
have made it from the orchards of Carinthia to
a café in Denver, splitting a bagel, watching the
shift in seasons defrock the trees.

An image queen, a vampire of attention, the fall
as you like to call it is more obvious than that
fine line in the waiter's accent, where we sit in
intrigue, wondering if, with his cured meats, our
neighbour will be blessed with dairy or the
second coming of our Lord.

Thrown

I missed Ireland tonight,
only when the bartender filled a
Guinness glass flat down,
even abandoned it to check an ID
and take another two orders,
tattoos crawling off both arms
like ivy down two mottled drainpipes.
On calling my second beer, he winked
and told me this one was on him.

Thrown, I remembered my first
man-to-man episode —
walking down St. Mary's Road
he asked if I was game
and I assured him I certainly wasn't,
but wanted to hug him for consideration,
squeeze him and assure him
it was going to be alright,
run my fingers through his crop in

a fatherly way and take two *hurleys*
and a *sliotar* down to the strand.
I wanted him to believe my naivety
like I believed his sincerity.
I pushed the boat out and wished too
for a large moon in a clear sky as
night slid its burlap sack over our
heads; like a dimmer switch in a bar
turned down in the sudden doubt.

Pleasure in its merciless forms

1.

Spent, sprawled sideways across the bed with
knees dangling over the edge, it could be said
that I was a drowned man bobbing on the
surface of the water.

I had heard sirens on the way down, seen
a woman reach for my thrashing arms to slowly
bring them to a halt and tasted sugar on my lips
when I stopped anticipating salt.

2.

Perhaps I am I lagging behind, or have become
detached as I wait in line muttering pleases and
thank yous on behalf of those in front.

In the parking lot, I watch as the mist rolls down
the San Gabriel Mountains like an avalanche
resolute on burying the cars below.

3.

Left and right of me, dead commuters drifting by
as I float on my back staring at the sky for
some sort of message;

even a nod of the head to let me know it's alright
to be the only one smiling, to which my blue lips
would mouth my abiding manners.

Sirens

The thought does cross my mind, fleetingly,
almost on a daily basis, each time the sirens
thunder past, whether I have by a few minutes'
stroke of luck at a poor sod's expense avoided
a fatal accident.

In the Starbucks of the local convenience store,
twelve hopefuls sit nervously waiting for their
name to be called to the interview, jolting every
time the shop floor music is interrupted by
the brusque announcer.

I sit with my *doppio*, staring out across a sea of
fruit and vegetables, listening to the discounts
on offer, morbidly wondering if one day I will
burn, perhaps be cut in tact from the mangled
wreckage of my wife's car;

or if my name will be called somewhere else,
with a quiet lane leading to our door, as I peter out
away from the sirens, from these giant stores and
coffee bars where out of twelve disciples waiting,
only one will leave here walking on water.

North from Laguna Beach

1.

It feels a lot longer in kilometres; the metric system making
everything seem a lot faster, further away, more expensive.

And here we are again making a mockery of geography,
wishing our recent air miles could be ascribed to one company.

Driving north from Laguna Beach, the Pacific struggles to
sleep in the glare of the marauding metropolis around the corner:

It is Halicarnassus during a siege, abraded sketches of victors
and the dead; the colour of Antelope Valley in April; your

Lithuanian skin where the sun screen missed, or my cheeks
ablaze with guilt the first time we kissed in Vienna.

I was Orson Welles skulking in the shadows and you Alida Valli;
our time measured like footsteps advancing on Gethsemane.

2.

I have been drawing a window sill of basil, rosemary and chive,
painting over the *blu-tack* marks on the bedroom wall, watching

you time and time again; learning your habits, your sleep patterns,
imagining your stomach extend by its nine monthly chapters.

I have been nailing Hollywood signs to buildings we wish to claim,
masquerading as a local on streets where angry men lash out at

invisible foes to the amusement of children and the horror of mothers.
You are there every time, safe in my hand, holding on to me as

I hold on to you, my arm across the divide driving north from Laguna
Beach. Outside, the tableau of images reads like a contents page

to a book written with every metric mile; and the burning sky above
Los Angeles just gets brighter and brighter and brighter.

II

Vienna

Quiet but for us, the Danube's dim mirror was
disturbed in her sleep as we swam naked through
the shadows of the furs tilting in the clean
summer wind.

In Heldenplatz we hollered opera to the dome
and heard the sound of hooves in the echo; the
rapturous applause that time would later condemn
to silence.

We cut through Volkgarten to stop for a piss,
shouting from behind trees about poems that would
need to be written. If you were Gustav Klimt, then
I was Graham Greene in need of inspiration.

And by Christ I looked for inspiration. I looked up
and down Ringstrasse, through the bustling parks in
the first district, up and down the steps of the
metro at Neubaugasse.

I imagined naked the girl at the bar in Café Carina,
her skin surrendering tattoos her parents would
never have approved of. She lit a cigarette and
dressed herself in limits.

At the market I looked at the old men selecting eggs
as if their hands could see through the shells. I looked
at David Rynhart's fingers, gently picking strings
with the same selective deftness.

I helped you up a ladder onto a rooftop and watched
as you stood there, proud as a lighthouse, inspecting
the ferocity of morning blazing its westerly trail.
There were three of us there.

And I looked five years deep into Marie's eyes and got
lost until you pulled me back out. Do you remember
that Stephen? Do you remember that view with the
Danube stretching and waking not too far away?

I remember thinking the seasons are arriving later
every year, as if the world has been slowed by the
weight of graves. Or maybe she has simply become
tired of turning,

or lying awake though a night of endless alarms
that nobody bothers to turn off.

Hotel Corpus Christi

I am looking for colours in the
negatives of us,

for your imprint on the shroud
we slept on in the Hotel Corpus Christi,

for any reason other than no reason
to forget your iron tongue,

smudge the flipside of the coin.

I didn't have the stomach for breakfast,
nor the courage to shower,
believing the water would set me alight.

And I have been walking all day in a daze.
Reminds me of being fifteen.
Perhaps that first real hangover,
the black eye or the love bite flying
the flag of injudiciousness.

Neither the cango hammer's
                    incessant assault
nor the smell of welding from the
nearby construction site
have registered.

I have crossed and confessed to four districts,
seeking redemption from the streets,
from the plastic smiles of the whores
on the *Gürtel*,

from the non-stop erotic *kino* where
I stopped to seek the morsel of a god.

In that darkness I found humanity cowering,
pummelled back into its seat
by a stricture of sexy demons.

Afraid to look sideways, I closed my eyes.
I woke with you in the Hotel Corpus Christi
and gently lifted the shroud.

You were naked and I ran my hand
                    over your back,
as softly the first time
as it would be the last.

To exit this particular nightmare, please follow the illuminated floor panelling along the aisle

I can see it quite clearly, even if it's a bit grainy, as though it were filmed on one of those seventies cameras — the likes of which we watched Farrah Fawcett flick her hair and flirt; and there she is, gorgeous as an air hostess beside her Lee Majors, him with his hair parted to one side, both of them waiting for the flashes of press photographers the moment they step into a blizzard of confetti. There were no press photographers, of course, but the photographs were taken, printed, cropped and placed ever so deftly into a white-laced album, the bow tied to keep it closed and that is how it stayed.

At least three decades must have passed for me to be thumbing through the unmarked pages of this affidavit of affection, flick-animating the unknown couple through their I do's, down the aisle and out into the shiny decorated Ford Cortina; the black and white film preserving in a split second's flash the faces of faultless optimism. God knows how many years or decades of perusing people have passed contemplating who, if one, was the donor, and whether he or she will sleep tonight in the environs of this Saturday market, restlessly stirring every now and again to one of two particular nightmares.

Three Magpies

Just now, this Jewish cemetery
doesn't feel so old.
These young green saplings
are breathing stolen life into
old rocks.

Just now, this is a beautiful place
for an ignorant mind.

An elderly man lifts his aging
Jack Russell beyond
our approach.

"You see this part?" she says,
cordoning off a rough area with
her fingers.
"This was the part of the camp
for women and children."

I grow excited remembering
the recent birth of my niece.

We walk on, up the embankment,
over the horizontal grave stones,
past the disused rail house and
back out onto the road.
Beyond the dual carriageway
Krakow purrs in the
midday sun.

My ignorant mind is almost 29
and I wish for three magpies
for my birthday;
a girl on a bike with a basket;
perhaps a few beers with the boys,
or some other reckless abandon.

For which the city is above suspicion

This city is burning with beauty,
but lacking fire.
The last time I walked through this park
you tugged on my sleeve and
      didn't need to say anything more.
You were a blonde Holly Golightly
and I was an Irish Rick Blaine.
You poured the petrol and
      I lit the match.

The desire to torch my clothes after work
is now a distant memory.
Those sultry Viennese nights have quickly
          shed degrees.
On the frozen grass of Burggarten, the
crows pecking at the soil constitute no jury
as I put these streets in the dock and seek
a scapegoat for my self-reproach;

that for which the city is above suspicion,
for which it simply burns.

Sighisoara in mid-February

It was late when the tired regional train from Brasov
wrestled to a suffering stop, scattering a handful of
silhouettes along the shadowy platform.

From the window of the taxi, the old town rose eerily,
as if the disgruntled earth had mustered its might to
squeeze the buildings skyward.

We took turns in seeing who could find the closest
depiction of how the black and purple clouds
clung to the rooftops above us, and I think you won
with something like 'quilted'.

Suffice to say, we weren't looking to check into a
Hilton or anything snazzy, to be swathed by the finest
silk sheets as we lie and listen to hard snow escape
from the red-slated roof.

What couldn't, however, escape my mind were those
clouds, inhaling the lights below until they engorged
and wore their whirl of colours like the Roma on the
train; their children feverish and wide-eyed as they
leaned out of the open-door carriage filling their cheeks
with slices of Transylvania through the trees.

I'm not looking for a canvas to paint this memory on,
nor a piece of string to help, some years down the line,
retrace the steps we crunched through Sighisoara's
somnolent streets as our clumps and giggles trespassed
night's quilted silence.

Those with ears polite

Those with ears polite hear more
than others bells clanging in far-off
Mediterranean villages by
the sea,

on cider afternoons in the shade
the fading roar of traffic beyond
the rape;

the renaissance of well-being
dissolving into occasional silence,
or a static echo of far-off
shells

ripping limbs from torsos bound
for burial beneath crumbling churches
and mosques —

actions ordered, then denied; we wait
for progress to prove genocide, for weather
to bring us new conversations
and masks

to cover our blushing cheeks, to
veil our blistered eyes and focus
ears

on the far-off sound of shells tickled
by the tide as we spin sincerity web-like
between the cracks in the wall
waiting

for spring to vacate; for summer to
send its flies: alibis for something that
never happened.

The Ships of the Neva

1.

It is like the first day after the last day of war
and I am the lost soldier, long presumed dead.
I am Pushkin returning from exile,
   enough breath pent-up within
to blow the ships of the Neva seaward.

There are mirrors in the ice pools on the roads
and I am a ghost yet to be reflected.

There are eyes squinting and frowns below them,
a score of chary siskins amongst the poplars;
   each a charade of me
in my capricious form of fancy.

There are four archangels perched upon a telephone
wire, three ready for take-off; the other,
   to mewl upon a blazing cloud,
perhaps set alight this oblast.

This oblast is rich with blood. This oblast harbours
more than the ships of the Neva in its white sheets.
And I am crossing Anichkov where there are already
nine and twenty months of fire folded into the sky.
I feel nine ounces of bread in my hand and bruises
in my pocket ready for occasion.

I wish there were shoes in the shoe boxes that
   I am returning to maraud,
but there are not.

2.

Where in the shadows of these raw streets
                does love last longer than a flyer?
I see good-will gestures of ill-tempered men recanted,
fickle as a photograph of wind.
I see the smile return to the seraphim's face,
fugitive as a wave's raucous beauty.

I see oligarchs and otters fighting for power,
peasants and perch watching on, toothless.
I see the waving arms of history reduced
                to a nod
and wonder from whom are these tacit waters running
                if not God?

Come & Go

I could come here as a stranger and
begin in the yellow anorak of
a tourist tickled
by the July drizzle.

If I stayed a little longer
perhaps the obsequious souvenir sellers
would recognize
my smile and wave.

Then I would be here to
live, and pass my moments
at tables where coffee
comes to disappear,

writing letters home,
exalting my new home,
until the seasons come and go and
I reach my fifty-first year.

Maybe then I'd disappear and
I could come here as
a memory, penned by my
son at a table

where coffee comes to disappear
and July drizzle
tickles the anoraks
of others.

Caucasus

Northward, incessantly, the flickering gunnery rumbles,
Far off, like a dull rumour of some other war.

Wilfred Owen

On shingle of seashells &
Bullet shells,
Ghosts drift along the shore
Of the Black Sea.

Staring at red men, waiting for
Green men,
We drift across streets,
Impassive,

Sit in smoke-filled corners
Of cafés,
Talk,
Write,

Push Pushkin into
Vacant mind space,
Prostitute prose for the
Glory of print,

Suck permeable plans of desire
Through filters, blow
Contrition into
Children's eyes,

Retreat once more
To Tammerfors
Where drunken talk
Of a Revolution

Spills from the
Pussy Cat Club on
A frozen back
Street while we

Simper with Bourgeois
Morals, bound
By the mental contraception
Of tradition.

In the dying distance,
A school bell sounds.
Shots are fired.
Sirens ring, cameras roll.

We can breathe with ease

We can breathe with ease poetry into the
sundry shades of red burning in
the skies over Gaza, perhaps likening
them to a pomegranate ripped open.

Ripe to write, I can't.
I can only watch as you sleep,
naked and foetal as you face the window.

And this womb of Connemara sky has
pulled for us its awning of stars high
above the spectre of the Bens and down
to Cromwell's Sound.

This sky is the Atlantic's appointment
and knows nothing of a night bombing.

It knows nothing of the upturned eyes
beneath, tearing its torso with fear.
It does not know that you are sleeping.

And I am no longer the writer of
footballs and broken windows.
I am not the cartographer of guilt.
Tonight, I am the prudent recluse,
the Bog Man returning to the bog,
the wind that need not wake you.

Eva at a safe distance

Eva always sits at a safe distance, three seats back,
hands under the table and shoulders pushed forward
like a schoolgirl whose mind is elsewhere.

When prompted, she speaks without breath, the odd
verb conjugation out of kilter, but otherwise voluble —
spurred by my pseudo nods of interest.

I feel guilty about the latter, curtaining off my mind
from her harmless rambling, fumbling my way through
the remaining hour of our class with questions I had
probably asked a few weeks prior.

Eva sits like a newscaster, reading off the teleprompter
immediately to my left; doesn't miss a word, holds
the same tempo, and be it a lottery win or a car bomb and
its ensuing carnage, her delivery is consistent.

To her I must seem vacant, like one those stern Soviet
border guards she flirted with in her youth; a face like a
weather forecaster announcing six days of rain.

The Widow

Brasov

There is a man in the window of the café,
     looks tortured, as if
searching for an algorithm in the rain, or
choosing a name for his unborn.

History, he thinks, can be a cruel bastard,
but we all know that.
Some will grit their teeth on
     being reminded;
others will feign ignorance as they
lift the rug of Europe and
     sweep the dust under Germany.

The rain is intermittent,
     the streets of Brasov quiet,
his face unaffected by the forthcoming
anniversary.

Vienna

Down by the fountain, in the sun,
     the sought-after tables are always in the shade
where the magazine sellers are relentless –
here, an elderly immigrant put a rose in my hand.

Twenty years since the Wall came down;
since, as a child on Christmas Day,
     Ceausescu keeled over on my television set.
We deliberately cut the knees out of our jeans
and taped Sinead O'Connor off the radio.

In Museum's Quartier I considered the rose,
     the widow in her mantle of repose,
and wondered how far we had come.

III

Do not compare the darkness

"I break the night, burning chalk
for the firm notation of a moment"

Osip Mandelstam

Do not compare the darkness to the night,
nor to its fair of clarity that we celebrate
sense by sense with hooded shadows and
their mute confusion, with the trickling
water of the ditches murmuring your epitaph,
with the wind spinning Ariadne's thread
through a choir of trees.

Tonight I am writing for you the largesse
of the lane upon the very steps that my god
treads.

Black as pitch, the western road at midnight
brings me back to Cahergal* and the lassitude
of an eighties summer where you would sit
on a fish box, patiently caulking the boat.
If you were Daedalus back then, then I was
your creation: both son and labyrinth from
which you would not escape.

On the far hill, a farm's yard light smashes
into the sky, oyster-white. I note the moment
and walk on.

* Cahergal is a townland in West Cork, Ireland.

Through windows dimly lit

Burren-grey, the sky through sky lights
is cigarette ash smashed across July.
The towns pass in half-eyed glimpses,
Inishannon, Bandon and Clon,
each address in its neon gown of auburn
as evening lights up and takes another drag.

Correct me if I'm wrong, but these roads
have widened and the journeys made longer.
These trips, these ritual returns, back down
where, as teenagers, the men we hated drove
Mercs and we hitching between the showers.

I remember the power cuts, the dark nights
through windows dimly lit by candles as wind
kept the boats tied up and the pockets dry.
I remember the colour of the grass after the
fish boxes were moved, watched the sky for
signs; helicopters from the trees come autumn.

Parliament Bridge

for Paul Solecki

At least you're fucking Irish he said, eyes
Beamish-black, a face that reminded me
of Andy Townsend for no other reason
than his was the first face that came into my
head as I tried my best to avoid eye contact.

The city's full of them foreigners now he
said, wiping thirty years of stout from his upper
lip. They wouldn't be long adding up at only
2.85 a pint and that, for sure, was neither his
first nor his last tonight.

I wanted to tell him that I was English; a tan
he might say; that I was born in the Midlands;
that my flesh and blood was as alien to Cork
as Warsaw to Brooklyn. But he was more
concerned with me throwing myself off of
Parliament Bridge.

Have you enough money? I had. And then he
talked about wealth and the sacristy of land
and suddenly I was unsure as to whether his
face now reminded me of Andy Townsend
or Genghis Khan.

Too depressed he said, and I was wearing
sandals. But sure wasn't the weather mighty
as the full moon keeled over in the sky
laughing off any advance dawn
might be planning. Still plenty of time for
me to throw myself off of Parliament Bridge

only to end up in a John Spillane song a few
years from now, or a Billy Ramsell poem,
where the hero is not me, but he who hauls
my bloated corpse from the water at Union
Quay. And sure if I died here tonight, bury me

beneath these old creaking floorboards so I can
lie and listen to men like him craft cavalries
from nights spent on park benches in London,
from all the bricks that have bent his back,

from the misfits of the Irish economy who
would look at the man sideways for talking
to me as I stop to admire the flicker of the
South Channel from the wall of Parliament
Bridge.

A Fire Escape in Brooklyn

1. Benevolence

He dropped ten euro onto the bar floor and
my conscience got the better of me.
"Thanks very much, you're a sound man, where are ya from,
thanks a million young man, where are ya from, aren't youse
the honest type? Fair fuckin' play to ya!"
He must have shaken my hands eleven times in two minutes.
On discovering you were from LA, he said the only
time he'd consider visiting was if he were flying over it
in a bomber.
I shook his hand one more time, wishing I'd kept my trap shut
and pocketed his fuckin' money.

2. A Serenade

Commuters are scared of each other, always sitting separately
and never leaving two seats together for couples.
You on one side of the aisle, me on the other, choosing the
alcoholic with the naggin of Jameson who wasted no time in
pointing a yellow-tipped finger in the direction of Glasnevin.
"That's where The Luke is buried," he said, breaking into
the first verse of Raglan Road.
A lump of a woman taking up four seats with bags hissed a
shush in his direction. I wanted to leave my seat and shush her.
In between the first and second verse he told me of his time
running the bar of The Buffalo in Camden Town where a
young Freddy Mercury once frequented – "a fine fellow,
great set of lungs, up to your shoulders so he was, lovely chap,
a gay individual mind you, but really nice, couldn't fault him."
He broke into the second verse as the train neared Leixlip
much to the vexation of that lump of a woman,
interrupted only by another swig of whiskey.

3. Come on, we're fine

I too have sung for you Raglan Road wandering up the back
lanes of West Cork under the fire blanket of a night cloud
where the oaks aligned the lane as still as ninjas and the beech trees
jingled in the breeze like belly dancers darned with tiny symbols.

You had never seen darkness like that before, and clutched my
hand out of sheer fear.
I wasn't quite the ghost of Luke Kelly but for all you cared
I could have been singing Radio Ga Ga.
Brushing a cold sweat from your forehead, I leaned in
and kissed you where I thought your mouth was.

4. Achill Island

"Aren't we fierce lucky with the weather?" came the
rhetoric from the woman in the sports shop with teeth
worthy of insurance,
as she scanned through your wellies,
rain mac and my gortex windproof waterproof
ultra lightweight breathable motherfucker of a jacket.
Fierce lucky my hole.

We set out for *Cuan na Coime* under a charcoal sky,
the forecast springing no surprises for the west of
Ireland in late August.
You looked gorgeous – a windswept gorgeousness –
while I looked indisputably slipshod.
Above us, the clouds rebuked by the mountains
loitered in uncertainty like dirty scolded dogs.

5. A fire escape in Brooklyn

You carried sand everywhere for a week; in your pockets,
the turn ups of your jeans, your purse, the seams of your jacket.
I had pictured for a long time our footprints on the sand
of Dog's Bay; thought forward with giddiness to the day when
we could park up the car and trespass its blanket of shells.

That all seemed a long way off in a cheap musty hotel room
in Amsterdam, washing your neck with a wet towel, asking
you to imagine the sensation beneath your feet walking across
the empty strand, to tell me how cool the breeze was and what
it felt like against the white cardigan you were wearing;
to touch the dew collected in the marram and wash the sand
from your hands; to count the lights on in the houses dotted
along the coast and to picture those sleeping inside.
It was at this point you closed your eyes and slept, unmindful
of the din and the smell of hash rising up from the café downstairs.

It seems a long way off now too, on a fire escape in Brooklyn,
counting the rungs to the ground, humming the tune of Raglan Road
to myself, as the words have got jammed behind my teeth,
as words so often do.

The Only Straight Man on Christopher Street

for Niall Connolly

Probably Puerto Rican, those three plumpish ladies with
pencilled-on brows, talking sideways out of eyes nibbling
away at the surroundings, their down-turned mouths just
about breaking lipstick on a bench on Christopher Street.
Here, the conscience of God does not sit and look out at
the world through windows, not at all. It wanders the street,
crosses on a red, cadges cigarettes at subway stops, buys a
slice to go, gets irritated when asked for ID at liquor stores,
gets caught looking at a passing girl's legs but smiles wryly
with the estimably bold thought of *look what I have created*.
On the sidewalk two men entwined in a slow dance take the
shape of an ampersand tempting others to do a Gene Kelly
as they pass. I follow the footsteps of Christknowswho, as
we all do, neglectful of the rumble of a train underfoot, the
gust of a passing bus, the face scrunch of the puzzled child
thrown by the transgenders, the ensemble of sirens calling to
each other on any street at any time where the conscience of
God is restless, and my acquisitive mind empty as the wombs
of nuns knelt in tacit prayer, hell-bent on His second coming.

A man with bleeding hands

A man with bleeding hands at the back door of *Out of the Closet*
this morning asked me for the bride and groom figurines at the
top of my donation box to put on the grave of his recently married
sister. He was topless, wore skateboarder jeans and hid what was
left of his shrunken skin behind an eddy of venous blue tattoos.

Impulse almost succeeded in steering me clear of his sanguine arms.
But who was I, making a donation, to doubt him, to dismiss his story
and bracket him on account of his homelessness? I watched as he
inspected his bounty, the plastic case unopened, his blood in the hot
midday sun running softly off the white exuberance of the dress.

Q on a triple letter square

for Nicolas Madigan

When you texted to say you were in the Bog
because the Shouty Man was setting up in Knockers,
I realised we might just have had as many codes
as POWs planning a tunnel.

Weather permitting, we'd be outside on Cross Street,
smiling in wonder at whether the non-attentive sipper
had noticed the pigeon shit in their Guinness,
or if the smell of turf through autumn's wet cement
had registered on anyone but us.

Perhaps we'd be somewhat sensitive at times like this to
that five-year-down-the-line thought,
stacked deep as kegs in the mind's cold room.

And didn't we word those streets like a Scrabble board,
finding the lexis as we went, sometimes stuttering,
other times free flowing and cavalier,
strolling past the pier and its quiver of swans,
with talk of future queens, of lands to conquer,
articulate as landing that 'q' on a triple letter square.

Perhaps it's easy to look back and be sentimental now,
you from your throne, me from mine –
a small sideways smirk escaping as subtly as that one
prisoner nobody thought would make a run for it.

Gower Street, 2am.

What do we hear before we sleep? Two spent lovers
curled into their nakedness, playing tennis with a yawn,
the post coital wetness on their thighs, sighing as they
shut their eyes to hear a police helicopter scour the hills,
searchlights ablaze; a rustle of sheets, their lips drying,
gurgles of the stomach not yet acknowledging its fast,
the occasional shift of legs or awkward repositioning
of that one odd arm. One lover watches the other doze
for a while, smiles at their unguardedness, the veracity
of skin that only a child blind to onlookers could carry.
A cricket outside the open window is metronome to
her pulse while a neighbour's bathroom lamp through
the atheistic silhouette of the trees is just a blink in the
inky black night where someone is still on the run.

Ghetto Birds

There were always palpitations,
Oftentimes a momentary shutdown
In the chest,
All sound drowned
Out by the roar of rotor blades above.
Some were even seen to bless themselves,
Saw it as impending news of the dead –
A capsized yacht, or worse:
A sunken trawler's crew of fathers
Five miles south of the Galley Head.

Here, there is only frustration,
Woken in the cold hours
By the ghetto bird circling,
Nose tilted towards the prey,
Patient as a seagull
As the morning grows shorter;
No compassion, pity, nor sign of the cross
For the soul caught in its spotlight,
Fighting
To keep his head above water.

Jungle of the Bourgeois Pig

for Denisa Duran

Your father talked me down from a high window ledge
the morning he lit a cigarette in the kitchen, poured
me cold coffee, and told me of how alien it felt to have
had the freedom to lie in the grass in a park in Vienna.
This choice of action is something I'd never thought of,
like so many things I have taken for granted to date.
I furrowed my brow and jiggled memories in my head
looking for a comparison to believe in when I heard
you recite to your court at Café Kafka the feeling you
had, and the watchful eyes upon you, the first time
you tasted a banana. Those of us in attendance smiled
as we looked for the comedy in such an odd situation,
conned by every thin comparison that sprung to mind.

We are watered down by choices, caught pants around
our ankles at a crossroads with no signs, every day staring
inanely at giant menu boards and convincing ourselves
that an iced lemon mocha with whipped cream and vanilla
is just what the doctor ordered. We have no use for effort
like we have no use for maps, our geography beamed from
satellites to the palms of our hands or to whatever jungle we
choose. And I am blown away by distance, sitting listening
to a man from Moldavia recant for me his translations of
Eminescu in a bar in Los Angeles, the clientele shrill as an
orchestra tuning up; his index finger pendulating gracefully,
assertively, as if a flouted conductor's baton.

No access to the Hollywood Sign

Everyone on Beachwood has a dog.
There is never parking.
The dogs are almost always small and yap
in the hours when most wish to sleep.
If there is parking, it's because there's
street cleaning the next morning.

One of these afternoons I will get lucky
and park on a small dog.
I will casually get out of my car, lock it,
and stroll off in my air of nonchalance.
The owner of the dead dog will be too
engrossed with a smart phone to notice.

The sign that informs tourists that there is
no access to the Hollywood Sign is the
most ignored sign in the whole of Los Angeles.
The morning after the rain, I sit outside
slicing strawberries into my Special K
watching tourists pose for photographs.

Satisfaction and beauty go hand in hand,
encouraging the Jacarandas to defy the
street cleaners and casually cast
their purple confetti across the sidewalk,
down onto the parked cars, the dogs,
the tourists rebelling against the signs.

How to kill a pig

I expected them to tell me that my bacon
had come from a happy pig, one that had had a full life,
was corn fed and had free range, did yoga in the mornings,
played the cello, spoke Latin and learned
to salsa dance while visiting relatives in Cuba.
I thought maybe there would have been a photo album
to accompany the sacrifice, documenting its first birthday,
first snow and first of everything else,
here an oink, there an oink.

In far corners, I dubbed the mouths of others,
their new voices outbattling the clattering gunnery of plates
slamming down organic everythings.
I gifted one woman berating her phone the French language
to make her all the more endurable.
Sweet as raw cane sugar to my fair trade coffee,
I had the young couple across from me nattering fondly
from their deathbeds; their soon-to-be-left world
better off now than it was when they were younger.

The child in the high chair wanted in on the action,
breaking into *L'enfant et les sortilèges* when faced
with a spoonload of non-GMO beige matter.
I used a sortilege of my own in stripping the walls clean
and emblazoning the newspaper headlines all
over them to see if anyone would notice, remark, question
that one glaring absence as Truth was led out the back,
strung up by its hind legs, throat slit, left to hang there
until the last drop of blood spattered into the bucket.

IV

Mrs. De Florian looks through
a north-facing window

for Lois P. Jones

> *"...perhaps the flight*
> *of the bird you wound remains..."*
>
> Rilke/What survives

Mrs. De Florian looks through a north-facing window,
as she has been doing every day for seventy odd years,
early spring sunlight piercing her bunker of trees.
She is cleaning as usual, paranoid about precluding fruit flies
and of course the dust.
The years though have become difficult to please,
weighted by wonder, etched in grey; each decade to her dismay
vanishing like startled starlings
into the unease above the glassless Sainte-Chapelle.

In this the delicate memory through which the birds haunt
the light, she knows she was not wounded by a rush of blood,
but rather by the flight.
She might think of tree-lined boulevards rapturous in spring's
unfurling yawn; Paris lying on its back dissecting the skies
as the wind breathes its encore of snow.

Summerfield Road

Were you to land me back there now,
cast me amongst the swansongs on the Anker
where two sides of the town draw
         blood from the same vein,

and the chimes of St. Editha's rise above
the viaduct, you would not notice my candour
as I drift down Summerfield Road.

Where the labyrinthine estates eat into the rape fields
of Drayton, the old keep eyes of young;
the snow dome, the cinema, the bowling alley;
each roundabout leading onto a roundabout.

There, through the brick lanes and ivy-clad walls,
names of Edden, Tricklebank and Hall
         fade into thickening bark;
playgrounds of four generations on indifferent
as the camera moves away overhead –

     the satellite image retracting on screen,
or a rootless eye glancing, furtively, once.

Worry about it tomorrow, do.

1.

Today, I found myself sitting on
some steps
      opposite a gay sauna
      on La Trobe Street,
writing postcards and
lying through my teeth;
      but the steps were a good
      place to view the 'Batman
Building' roaring above Elizabeth
Street and the
      steadfast flow of commuters
      of whom I am now jealous.

2.

Two years ago in Shanghai,
I saw buildings as big as
my ambitions.

Today, I was unsure whether these
buildings speaking to me were saying
"Go find a job" or
"Go find a god."
Worry about it tomorrow, do.

Between now and my uncertain exit

Between now and my uncertain exit, there
are probably ninety-nine poems I will write
and one, please God, that I will never be
entirely satisfied with.

This would be the one about your jacket,

the one that was too heavy to carry and
ended up on a park bench in North Beach,
Christmas come early to the homeless man
quickest out of the blocks.

He will tell you a jacket will keep the shape of
your body long after you have left it –
why, then, should my mind be any different?

There are some, though, who will forget you and
others who, through the iris of memory and
the snapping of fingers, will slowly reassemble
your intricate image.

They will see you turn the stiffest of necks as
you enter the bar, leather-booted beautiful;
your bottom lip pursed to coax my smile.

They will see Christ taken down from the cross;
you, dead to the world on the couch,
closing your eyes to John Martyn or inhaling a
night that has forfeited reason for your comfort.

And everything is the same here.
The summer has outrun us all again, gone before
we have taken our chance to swim;

gone before the tables outside Neachtain's
have been brought back in. Gone, somewhere
south of Fastnet as we murder pints and count
the pay days until Christmas.

And the walls of The Crane still sweat on Saturday
nights where Stephen and I still spout poetry to
strangers and, as I write, Nick and the Atlantic are
cooking up storms.

Some nights, kept awake by the racket of teenage
drinkers breaking bottles off the wall of the new
museum, I imagine slipping beneath the Corrib with
you,

lying there and listening to the sound of
the water rushing over us,
the whole world rushing over us,
that dark night on a country lane in Kent,
that concert in Webster Hall rushing over us,
that Kris Kindle I couldn't figure out;

that patch of grass in St. Kilda watching fireworks
fizz and crackle over the city;

that fucking airbed in a tent at Wilson's Prom
and the waves that smashed me around
good and proper: the stubborn Irishness in me
that kept coming back for another beating
and loving it;

those quiet weeks rushing over us;

Monday evenings in Cape Lounge and
the 119 rushing over us;

that night in a warehouse in Brunswick
staring through the green glass of empty
bottles of wine, remembering the night
before when you told me you would always,
always remember it,

my fingers through your hair,

making love to the sound of the winter wind
sneaking in through the gaps in the corrugated roof;

that pile of leaves halfway up Nicholson that
I dumped you in;

that night I pretended to have locked myself
out so as only to sleep on the floor below your
bed, imagining the homeless man who, beneath
your jacket, was now sleeping in North Beach
with both the smell of your hair
and the rain in Galway,

and can you imagine missing the rain?

Missing it like the café tables in Tallinn where
I sat sipping a silent amen ready to swim the Gulf
of Finland;
like the soft crunch of frosted grass underfoot
marching to the British Lookout with a five
year-old soldier;
like that north I once traded for the south;
like the view across the water from Kowloon on
a balmy night in April;
like the ripples in the South Channel walking

towards Parliament Bridge tearing strips
out of the silence because we were drunk and
no-one else seemed to care;
like the hours I entertained in Café Europa
scared shitless of the spring and wondering if,
one day, I would regret what I was about to write
or regret my decision to leave it all behind.

And I wonder again about your jacket
and if it still remembers you,
and if someone is still touching its dark fibres

like fingers remembering hair.

After the Thaw

You will learn not to be disappointed
now that you have weathered the stares.
You have mapped footprints to floorboards,
followed them to the door, and
now imagine two more, tiny
and awkward as the final fall of snow
regaled by restless earth.

I can see you tonight, your smile aglow,
your belt made of shells;
the opacity of five rabid years becoming
clearer in the winelight.
You are musing over some intricate detail
of your latest sketch: the shading, the
contrast; perhaps fearful of its completion.

I imagine instead that you are enamoured
by the stock doves returning to the sky
and its forthcoming light of transparent depths.
And you are walking now, beneath fidgety
birches, through grass wet with vernal dew.
You stop by the lake at the edge of the
wood and draw comfort from the thaw.

Thought Bubble for the Unobserved

My accent doesn't carry well over a milk steamer,
beside a man in shorts, pulled-up white socks and
New Balance running shoes and him shouting at a phone.
Another customer dressed as a train conductor orders
a tea that nobody's ever heard of while clutching a
book that nobody's ever read. I end up with a coffee
I didn't request and a friend I didn't necessarily want.

We all dread those moments from time to time – the
where-are-you-from bait we bite at to be reeled into
the genealogy of a complete stranger who has never
set foot on the island of his ancestors. I watch with
curiosity the Hispanic lady cleaning the tables, mutely
gliding from one corner to the next, invisible as a
long-standing memory better off kept that way.

Clear as my conscience may be, you still haunt me as the brown settles to black

sit there and recommence as if nothing had ever happened,
your hands conducting the orchestra of your purity.

Yet now, we are at the age, it seems, where clichés suffice to
regale the years and talk of how kind they have been,
naivety a scapegoat for the slips.

The child in me wants to take you down, come up with
some playground retort to send you packing;
the man in me wants to feel nothing,

sit and run my finger down the side of my pint glass,
and look straight through where the dark stuff used to be.

Sundial

Restiveness grants reprieve for your unutterable name,
      exile but a narcissistic luxury.
Waking to a stone against my bedroom window,
I see your face, hangdog in the light of the porch.
We hitchhike out to Roundstone under a mussel-blue sky,

the tincture of Connemara barely batting an eyelid
      beneath its westerly spread, the seagulls riotous
in their air of we-know-something-you-don't-know;
the Atlantic a clumsy emissary,
crashing like a brass band down a stairwell.

I take a black and white photograph of you on grey sand –
an unintentional sundial, back to the camera;
      staring out to sea as if waiting for an allied assault,
or a man holier than I to part the waves and cut you a path
to a belated promised land.

V

The Quarry

Chrisht, we won't have a bob at all! Junior proclaimed,
the last three words of his declaration rolling out as one.
It had become everyman's catchphrase on wet days,
peering out from a rusting metal container unit at the
disembowelled stomach of wet rock.
Sinners did not pick stones in the rain,
which is why we wouldn't have a bobatall.

No posters of Rita Hayworth adorned the walls of
our asylum, and every coming Saturday night
felt more like the chalky promise of parole.
That summer took longer than most: ten hours a day
knelt in prayer with hammer and stone, feeling no
remorse at using the Lord's name in vain every time
the chisel slipped; broken scabs on bloodied hands
as if two nails had been driven into each.

Wouldn't *himself* be along shortly though, over the brow
of the hill in his new Pajero, stone mad, blaspheming the
Trinity to find out why we weren't on our knees?
He would sure, and by God we'd tell him where to
go with his *productivity* and he wouldn't be long buzzing
up those electric windows, driving off, out the gap.

Chrisht, you'd catch your death in that! Junior decreed
in an act of unparalleled ventriloquism,
his mouth combating both a swig of Lilt and a Fig Roll.
This was not a scene scripted by Stephen King nor was it
a movie narrated by Morgan Freeman, and it didn't
matter a shite to Junior that he wasn't Andy Dufresne
quarrying himself to some eventual freedom.

Istanbul

They are plastering on lipstick in pay-to-enter toilets
around the corner from the mosques, where old men
sit on back streets selling toilet seats, spices by the
shovel, flashlights, and Audrey Hepburn t-shirts;
the city going about its day like a petulant child,
pushing us on impatiently, racing ahead and turning
back to beckon us to catch up, to buy whatever it points
at, to stay up late with us and tug at our shirts to the
extent that we take refuge in a café across the bridge
from the Grand Bazaar to watch the helium moon float
and burn above the Bosphorus while murmuring a prayer
to the Marmara or to whatever god is above us that we'll
sleep with the belief that we had found something new.

Our precious measured days

My survival is a quick glance across at a Frenchman
embracing his English girlfriend in a bar on the
Upper East Side, and I close my eyes.

It's top down and Sunset Boulevard in light traffic,
cutting across Fountain to save time,
       palm trees lofty as we are ambitious with
our precious measured days.

It's August and you and I are nipping at the heels of Berlin,
harrying its streets with drag-along suitcases and
faces that would suggest arousal.

These cities lift their skirts to us you see, show us a little
bit of leg, a stiff nipple;
       dry ride us to the brink of climax and then walk away
waving their hands in the air in a protest of innocence,
nothing to see here, keep moving along.

On a bridge in Regensburg

To hear my name, called out across the Roman stones on a
bridge in Regensburg through the languid March drizzle,
was to breathe again as my head burst through the water.

Two lovers in the corner of the Black Bean café exchanged
mocha tongues and disregarded censorious onlookers;
me with an envious pang of I've-worn-that-t-shirt as I passed.

I have for too long been hitchhiking in the opposite direction
to which the world is going, malingering through the medium
of other people's beds, but more often their couches.

This incessant journeying, these photographs that document
the ages of my illusory face, this cracked black pepper light
on my skin at night is just a stopgap grace.

On a bridge in Regensburg, my head bobbed up when beckoned
and, for a second, I was home again; a mother's call from the
kitchen door to a boy and his dogs just two fields away.

Dark Counties

Now that helicopters are as pertinent as the
kaleidoscope of starlings over the lake,

I tend to think of you more often,

how, despite a distance measured more in years
than in airline miles and Christmas visits,
you still conjure up with ease the brilliance that
suffuses the romance of my suffering memory.

Dear island, dear battered rock:
I had come here to be pestered by nostalgia,
entrusting the list of malts to whisk me off
to the turf outside their distilleries,
to feel falsely at home in those dark counties,
a chimney-stained inhale of villages lock-doored
at dusk; a still silver night on a boreen in West Cork —
the moon like a sipped-at pint of Murphy's.
My father is on a trawler heading out past the Stags,
every bit as alive as the wind ripping into the Storka.

There's a house out past the church, beyond the lake,
untended grass, knee-high hiding buoys,
the garden letting itself go as we have ourselves
in these months undone by the gales,
while down at the water, our boat clings to the pier,
back to the whip of the wind, greeting its
lashes like a martyr true to the cause.

Dear island, dear battered rock:
Do you remember me at all?
Until now I have addressed you with grace,
leaned favourably towards any recant of your devilment,
regaled five continents with clichés of your valour.
Until now, this has been about me;
about the dead I never buried, the Band-Aid metaphors,
the narcissism of my exile.

If I believed, I'd bury instead these lines,
eight feet deep and light a candle for each;
sweep all our disagreements under a concrete slab,
just like you did;
rattle the beads if any fucker came near me.

Dear island, dear battered rock:
the fugitives amongst us quantify longing through
our fervent exchange of letters, breathe your sea
breezes through a trove of photographs.

Our murmuration is less spectacular from this distance;
colliding in the scope of spotlights,
or braking trains shrill as unfed seagulls,
or a chorus of voices somewhere beyond the blades,
the grain, the lake.

Welcome to Kiribati

i.m. Dennis O'Driscoll

When I hear the passive euphemism of
         'the death has taken place',
it makes me think it has all been organised, staged;
that the man in question is far from dead
and instead disembarking a plane in a straw hat
reading a sign that says *Welcome to Kiribati*.

We back home don doleful faces, pasting
         micro-obituaries in irreverent places with
well thought-out testimonials gracing the paper
and screen, while he collects his belongings at
the baggage carousel, smiles as he breezes through
passport control and walks towards the light.

A year down the line and we might find ourselves
         congregated to mark his anniversary,
dribbling poems and bleeding songs; others amongst
us even bowing heads to repent, nervous of who
might be next – the old, the clumsy, the obvious or
that quiet chap in a suit standing under the exit sign.

Photograph: Sascha Osaka

NEIL MCCARTHY grew up in West Cork in the eighties watching MacGyver and launching himself from trees on zip wires fashioned from old clothes lines. His sense of adventure followed him into his twenties when he graduated from the National University of Ireland, Galway, and began travelling and writing poetry soon after. He has so far featured as a guest speaker in literary festivals, conferences, fringe festivals etc. in Australia, the US, Ireland, the Czech Republic and Austria to name a few. In this time his poems have also appeared in dozens of international journals and anthologies, in print and online, and have additionally been translated and published in Romania, Serbia, and Hungary. He now lives in Vienna where he teaches English and still climbs the odd tree whenever the chance presents itself.

www.neilmccarthypoetry.com

Salmon Poetry gratefully acknowledges the support of
The Arts Council / An Chomhairle Ealaíon
towards the publication of this book

www.**salmon**poetry.com

"Like the sea-run Steelhead salmon that thrashes upstream to its spawning ground, then instead of dying, returns to the sea – Salmon Poetry Press brings precious cargo to both Ireland and America in the poetry it publishes, then carries that select work to its readership against incalculable odds."

TESS GALLAGHER